MIRACLES IN ESPANA

Faith Awakened in an Ancient Land

TERENCE LEWIS

WestBow Press books may be ordered through booksellers or by contacting:

WestBow Press
A Division of Thomas Nelson & Zondervan
1663 Liberty Drive
Bloomington, IN 47403
www.westbowpress.com
844-714-3454

Interior images: T.Lewis

• Scripture marked (KJV) taken from the King James Version of the Bible.
• Scripture marked (NKJV) taken from the New King James Version®. Copyright © 1982 by Thomas Nelson. Used by permission. All rights reserved.
• Scripture quotations marked (ESV) are from The ESV® Bible (The Holy Bible, English Standard Version®), copyright © 2001 by Crossway, a publishing ministry of Good News Publishers. Used by permission. All rights reserved.

ISBN: 978-1-6642-9541-4 (sc)
ISBN: 978-1-6642-9543-8 (hc)
ISBN: 978-1-6642-9542-1 (e)

Library of Congress Control Number: 2023905348

Print information available on the last page.

WestBow Press rev. date: 6/5/2023

WESTBOW
PRESS®
A DIVISION OF THOMAS NELSON
& ZONDERVAN

Contents

Preface

Setting: The primary focus of this story takes place during ten days in Spain from May 6, through May 16, 2002.

Theme: An adventure with God and His "Wondrous Love" in Spain.

Extraordinary accomplishments in a region ripe for revival.

Caveat lector: This account of our trip to Spain is taken mostly from my wife Carla's and my personal journals (2001 and 2002) and from our best recollection of the people and events depicted. Any mischaracterizations or inaccuracies here are truly unintentional. Hopefully, those involved will understand, and if necessary, contact the author and or publisher. Our goal here is to simply convey a series of what we believe were providential events. Relax and enjoy the trip!

> For the message of the cross is foolishness to those who are perishing, but to us who are being saved it is the power of God. (19) For it is written: "I will destroy the wisdom of the wise, And bring to nothing the understanding of the prudent."(20)…Has not God made foolish the wisdom of this world?…(25) Because the foolishness of God is wiser than men.(26) For you see your calling brethren, that not many wise according to the flesh, not many mighty, not many noble, are called.(27) But God has chosen the foolish things of the world to put to shame the wise, and God has chosen the weak things of the world to put to shame the things that are mighty; (28) and the base things of the world and the things which are despised God has chosen, and the things which are not, to bring to nothing the things that are, (29) that no flesh should glory in His presence. (1 Corinthians 1:18–29 NKJV)

Acknowledgments

Of course, the first person I'd like to praise and thank is the Lord our God, who prepared and called us at this time for this ministry. In the Bible, the book of Esther reads in part, "who knoweth whether thou art come to the kingdom for such a time as this?" (Esther 4:14 KJV).

Second, I'd like to thank my wife Carla and my son Elijah, one of God's miracles from Spain. You helped render this event with clarity of what I believe is foremost in God's heart: soul winning!

We also appreciate so much the support and encouragement of our good friends Pastor Kelly Isbell and his wife Esther. Tim and Karen Johnson from Bay City, Michigan assisted us as well.

Many thanks to all of our brothers and sisters in Christ and family members who prayed for us throughout the ten days we were in Spain.

Westbow Press Publishing Company, whose expertise solidified the quality of this account, deserves recognition.

Introduction

All through the history of the world, God has used various means to accomplish His tasks and to do His will, almost always through the agency of frail human beings. They may have been poor sojourners, prophets, priests, and kings, but compared to our sovereign, omniscient, omnipresent, omnipotent God, they were but "chaff that the wind drives away!" (Psalm 1:4 ESV). God chooses what, where, when, why, whom, and how as we His followers continue to learn over time and through experience. No excuses—just trust!

This was the case of my and my wife Carla's life. We had known the Lord since our younger days, and He used us in a variety of ways. Later in our lives, as we, I believe, became spiritually sensitive to His voice and presence, God chose to use us and six others uniquely at this special time.

1

Revealed Calling to Spain

When God speaks, trust and obey!

July 23, 2001

I've been praying to know more of the Lord's will and worshipping more effectively lately. This morning, while I was in the shower, singing and praying and seeking God, I told Him I would go wherever He wanted me to go. Much to my surprise, He spoke clearly in my mind and spirit, "Spain." I had no idea or hint of any kind where He wanted us to go. Right away, I told my wife Carla, and we discussed much, prayed much, and focused on this.

God doesn't reveal everything at once.

> Being confident of this very thing, that He who has begun a good work in you will complete it until the day of Christ. (Philippians 1:6 NKJV)

> Surely the Lord God does nothing, Unless He *reveals* His secret to His servants, the prophets. (Amos 3:7 NKJV; emphasis added)

> For you can all prophesy one by one, that all may learn and all may be encouraged. And the spirits of the prophets are subject to the prophets. (1 Corinthians 14:31–32 NKJV)

August 4, 2001

Later, on my lunch hour from work, I had my usual Bible study in the car. I was led to read in Acts 7 about Stephen's defense. Verse 3 stood out; God speaks to Abraham, saying, "'Get thee out of thy country, and from thy kindred, and come into the land which I shall shew thee'" (KJV).

August 13, 2001

I was working at Home Depot in Florida. This morning, I studied my Spanish. There were Spanish-speaking customers coming into my workplace, and I wanted to brush up on my Español.

August 23, 2001

It was an uneventful day at Home Depot, though I did manage to practice my Spanish with a customer.

Sunday, September 2, 2001

Carla, Ryan, Gene, and I went to early church. It was a very good message on Acts 7:3, the same text as my entry on August 4 about God's call to Abraham to leave his family and country. Yesterday, I was praying for more confirmation from God, and I believe today was His answer. Thank You, Lord!

Thursday, September 13, 2001

God gave me Psalm 138:18 this morning: "The Lord will perfect that which concerns me" (NKJV). Also, Philippians 1:6: "He will complete His work in us!"

Friday, September 14, 2001

While Dave and I went to the pharmacy in Stewart, Florida, I sat next to a lady and studied my Spanish book. She sounded like she knew Spanish, so I asked her a question about two words in the book that had the same meaning. After we talked, I found out that she was from Madrid, Spain. She told me all about Spain and Madrid. Last night, as we were watching the Christian TV station, they announced they were beaming their first European telecast to (guess where) Madrid, Spain! Thank You, Lord!

Wednesday, January 23, 2002

I dreamed I was in Spain. In my numerous Bible studies, I kept coming across verses like Romans 15:24, 28, and 29: "Whenever I journey to *Spain*, I shall come to you...Therefore, when I have performed this and have sealed to them this fruit, I shall go by way of you to *Spain*. But I know that when I come to you, I shall come in the fullness of the blessing of the gospel of Christ" (NKJV; emphasis added).

God gave many confirmations of our call to minister in Spain.

2

A Supported Mission

January 10, 2002
Vision of Jesus
After about four months of receiving signs, and four months prior to leaving for Spain, I experienced the most gloriously influential dream-vision I have ever encountered. I believe the Lord gave me this not only to equip me for Spain but to radically change my life forever. I am relating some of this from my journal, but not all.

In the dream, Jesus visited the earth and stayed briefly at the top of a mountain. People were coming to see him, but the whole world wasn't aware that He was there. Somehow, I made it there to see Him. At that time, He was sitting in a small garden. He looked at me face to face and gestured for me to come over to Him. As I approached Him, I grew younger and seemingly smaller, reminding me of Matthew 19:14 (KJV): "But Jesus said, 'Suffer (allow the) little children, and forbid them not, to come unto me: for of such is the kingdom of heaven.'" He had shoulder-length hair and wasn't radiating any visible glory, but the goodness and virtuous love around Him was indescribable—more than overwhelming!

He had me sit on His lap, and He put His arms around me in a big hug. Then He told me many things, and I asked Him things. He limited Himself to the natural laws of humanity. I cannot adequately describe my feelings and emotions during our conversation. They were extremely joyful and intense and I was totally encompassed with His presence. It was beyond overwhelmingly awesome!

After my encounter with the Lord, I gained a new perspective on life with insightful understanding on its priorities. Second Corinthians 5:17 says, "Therefore if any man be in Christ, he is a new creature" (KJV).

Now nothing fazed me but Jesus and the truth. No, I didn't become perfect, but I try to follow the one who is. My faith was transformed from religious and intellectual to relational and heartrending. Thank You, Lord, for Your gracious blessing. "Blessed is the man You choose, And cause to approach You" (Psalm 65:4 NKJV).

3

Good as Dead

Friday, March 22, 2002

I prayed in the middle of the night over half an hour. God gave me part of the verse Hebrews 11:12: "as good as dead." The whole verse is, "Therefore sprang there even of one, and him as good as dead, so many as the stars of the sky in multitude, and as the sand which is by the seashore innumerable" (KJV).

I believe this and the previous verses are telling me that when we go to Spain, we will win many souls.

4

Support from Church

For a few months, Carla and I had been sharing and praying with our Christian friends in Bay City, Michigan about our call to Spain. Many continued to remember us in prayer and some with financial support.

Around April 2, 2002, we were led to contact Anita Mahoney, enlistment assistant for IMB–SBC (International Mission Board Southern Baptist Convention). At this time, they were in the position to connect us with a mission group in Florida, who were planning a ten-day trip to Spain in May. We were informed of the cost for this excursion. It would be approximately $2,700.

I discussed our proposed Spain plans with our pastor at Riverwalk Baptist Church and said I would announce them on Sunday. That evening, Carla and I went to the coffeehouse (Bay City Coffee and Tea) run by Kelly's wife, Esther Isbell. I composed a rough draft letter to the Southern Baptist Association asking for funds for our trip to Spain.

5

Favor at Work

Later that morning, I talked to Chris, the manager at Home Depot in Michigan where I had just applied for a job. She said she had a job for me in the paint department. I told her I still needed Sunday morning off each week. She said, "Fine." I also informed her that I needed to take eleven days off in May to go to Spain. She said, "Wonderful!" Then she asked me how much I was getting paid before. I said, "Ten dollars an hour." She said, "I'll start you at eleven dollars an hour." Thank You, Lord!

6

Support from Friends

Jehovah Jirah, God Our Provider

Monday, April 8, 2002

Prayed in the middle of the night with Carla between 2:30 and 3:00 a.m. I read 2 Peter 1 and meditated on it. We found out at 12:50 p.m. that the total cost for the Spain trip is $3,150.00. I memorized John 3:16 in Español. Carla and I had lunch with Kelly and Esther at Bob Evans. They told us that yesterday in church, God had laid on the hearts of a couple to give substantially for the mission trip, and God told Kelly and Esther to give the rest of the amount needed for the trip! Thank You, Lord! They didn't know how much we needed, but God did, and He threw in an extra fifty dollars. Our God is an awesome God!

Tuesday, April 9, 2002

Dr. Shirley Martin, the leader of the mission team, left a message late. We read Isaiah 52; the focus was on verse 7.

Wednesday April 10, 2002

Carla and I had Team Kids ministry at church. We gave testimony about Spain. Later at the coffee shop, we viewed this week's video and guess what? It was about missionaries going to a Spanish-speaking country!

April 21, 2002

Journaled about relatives, along with Carla's ex-husband, unknowingly being used by Satan to oppose our trip to Spain.

God impressed upon me Colossians 1:13 tonight. At the church business meeting, Pastor Steve motioned the church to give Carla and me $200 for Spain. They unanimously agreed! Thank You, Lord. Later, we had good fellowship at the coffee shop.

Monday, April 22, 2002

We received our passports.

April 26, 2002

Home Bible study at 7:00 a.m. was very good. Carla, Tim, Karen, and I Sunday studied Acts 10. Carla knows John 3:16 in Español now. I almost have John 1:12 down pat.

7

Saga Revealed

Flight

Monday and Tuesday, May 6 and 7, 2002
Rushed around getting ready to go to Spain. The Isbells took us to the airport. We left Bay City, Michigan at 1:40 p.m., flew to Detroit, then to Amsterdam, then to Madrid. We arrived Tuesday at 9:30 a.m. We met six of our seven missionaries at the airport. They were Dana and Karen, Karla and her mother Ruth, Sandy, Shirley Martin, and our interpreter Keely.

A. Hotel

At Chamarti'n, the hotel we stayed in, we had a short informal training session, and then we were shown around. After a short nap, we all took a bus to central Madrid (SOL). It was very historical. All kinds of people were there.

B. Prayer

We split up and walked around the square of Plaza Mayor, praying silently and looking for opportunities to witness. I handed out five tracts and prayed for the recipients. One of the tracts was to a mother, Carmen, whose little girl, Selina, ran into my elbow just slightly. I apologized, and Selina grabbed my hand and didn't want to let go. I talked to them in broken Spanish, then Carmen said she knew English as she had spent ten years in Texas.

We had a good rapport and now we all are praying for their salvation. Carla and I walked to the middle of the square (Plaza Mayor) again. Long ago, many thousands of Christians were martyred as heretics. It seemed as if their blood was crying out from the ground, as the cobblestones there were still red. Later, we stood on the central point in Spain. We prayed for souls.

8

Spiritual Journey

Signs and Wonders

Wednesday, May 8, 2002
Back at the hotel. Prayed in the middle of the night at 3 a.m. to 4:05 a.m. for Madrid's souls, for strengthening and protection for our group, and for signs, wonders, and healing today. We prayed also for God to break down spiritual "principalities, etc. over Madrid and for one million souls to be saved in this area. Madrid for Jesus!"

Carla's Journal

May 8, 2002
Morning. I opened my Bible to the book of Isaiah. I read chapter 8 and God brought attention to verse 9, "Give ear all you from far countries" and verse 18, "We are for signs and wonders" (KJV). At about the same time, God gave Terry Acts 2, which is about God pouring His Spirit on all flesh, and prophesying. This includes "I will show wonders in heaven above and signs in the earth beneath" (KJV). Later that morning, Terry led our group in a devotional concerning Acts 2 again. Notice verses 19 and 43 signs and wonders. Verse 19 Peter was quoting Joel's prophecy and verse 43 a fulfilling of that prophecy.

Terry's Journal

May 8, 2002
Earlier in the a.m., Carla had read in her personal devotion Isaiah 8:9—"Give ear all you from far countries" (NKJV)—and verse 18—"*Behold, I and the children whom the Lord hath given me are for signs and wonders*" (KJV; emphasis added). Thank you Lord! We didn't tell each other what we were studying until after the fact.

Later, our group prayer walked in and out of the city near Retiro Park (huge). We handed out tracts, etc. I handed one to a lady who ran a newsstand and told her in Español, (with the help of Keely), "Here, I have some *good* news for you." We then prayed for her. Later, we souvenir shopped. Then Carla and I joined Keely at her church, Immanuel Baptist, for their prayer meeting. It's an English-speaking church with many nationalities in their make-up. That night, there were three Caucasians (us), four Philipinos, two Ibereans, and one from the Congo.

We are all one in Christ Jesus! The prayer was great! At Carla's suggestion, we all laid hands on one young woman and prayed for her.

9

Spiritual Journey Continued

Wednesday, May 8, 2002
Signs and Wonders
Later: Carla and I went out for a late supper at Pepe's. The salmon was delicious. We split one order. I believe God gave me Isaiah 42:6, 7, 9, and 43:19.

"I, the LORD, have called thee in righteousness, and will hold thine hand, and will keep thee, and give thee for a covenant of the people, for a light of the gentiles, (7) to open the blind eyes, to bring out the prisoners from prison, and them that sit in darkness out of the prison house. (9) Behold, the former things are come to pass, and new things do I declare: before they spring forth, I tell you of them." (KJV)

"Behold, *I will do a new thing*; now it shall spring forth; shall ye not know it? I will even make a way in the wilderness, and *rivers in the dessert*." (Isaiah 43:19 KJV; emphasis added)

10

New Things

At first, I was believing that some thoughts in Isaiah along the lines of sin versus righteousness, captivity/addictions or enslavement versus deliverance and freedom, darkness versus light, salvation with newness of life in Christ, etc. were informing me that many souls would be saved in Spain and that happened. As I quoted earlier Amos3:7: "Surely the Lord God does nothing, Unless He reveals His secret to His servants the prophets" (NKJV).

> "The secret things belong to the Lord our God, but those things which are revealed belong to us and to our children forever. (Deuteronomy 29:29 NKJV).

It was soon revealed to us that, newness of life, a way in the wilderness and *rivers in the desert* also meant a healing of my *'dry waters.'* At this point in time, I was fifty-four years old and still unable to conceive children.

We believe God rewarded us by allowing Carla to get pregnant in Spain! He has a time and a place for everything, or as it is worded in Ecclesiastes 3:1, "To everything there is a season, and a time to every purpose under the heaven." "He hath made everything beautiful in his time" (Ecclesiastes 3:11 KJV).

11

Warfare and Prayer Warriors

May 9, 2002, Thursday
Prayed in the middle of the night about fifteen minutes, and was tired, as I went to bed at 2 a.m.

In the morning, mused through Isaiah. At 11:15 a.m., we all left to go prayer walking at a couple of parks. Then, we ate lunch at the world's oldest continuing restaurant, <u>Botin</u>. It's in the Guinness Book—very old-world looking. They had great food. Then, at my request, we went to Plaza Mayor and stood in the center (where many Christians had died) and prayed for God to "rend the heavens" and come down and bring revival and an awakening to Madrid and the surrounding area, to *cast out the powers of darkness and bring in the light of the glorious gospel of Christ*! Also prayed for many souls to be saved and victories won for Jesus and the Kingdom of God, and for it all to begin right there! Thank you Lord!

18

African Church

Later, we went to the city's only mosque and prayed for Christianity there. We had more prayer walking after this, quoting some appropriate scriptures. Still later: we went to this African immigrant church to do some prayer walking and met the pastor outside, Jean Simon—his card read Bayekula Ngimbi. We didn't know they were having their prayer meeting. The pastor invited us inside and we prayed with them. They were very friendly, joyful, warm-hearted people. The pastor has the gift of evangelism and seems to be a very spiritual man. He and his wife are from the Congo. He speaks French, English, and Spanish. Two of our ladies gave him a monetary gift so he could sell a CD which would enable him to preach and evangelize full time!

12

A Summary of Obedience

God chooses and enables us

When we believe and obey Him, our prayers will soon be heard, as we stand on His infallible word!

The humble child discovers love and grace; unimaginable miracles then take place.

Like a ship on a sunlit sea, God calls, chooses, and uses even me.

In my case, it was more than I could imagine or think.

Giving Spiritual/Tangible Food

After reading Proverbs 10 in the morning, we all went to the Spanish-speaking church, Ebenezer Communidad, to help distribute food to the immigrants, mostly Ecuadorians. We gave them new Bibles and were able to present the gospel to many of them. They were very open to the word, and many got saved! They would come in and sit down in small groups, one after another, and hear the message. I was able to share the gospel with my broken Spanish, the verses I had memorized, and help of the Nuevo Testimento (New Testament) in my pocket.

May 10, 2002 Friday a.m.

One group (fifteen or twenty people) would pray to receive Christ, led by an older Caucasian brother named Horace, or a similar name. He drove about two and a half hours to church every time he came. Soon, another group would come and sit, and we would start all over again. Thank you, Lord, for such an outpouring of your Spirit of liberty! One lady who keeps order and communication going in a dynamic way is also a doctor and dentist. The believers there are beautiful people. They give food out to over *1,500 immigrants each week!*

Comunidad Evangelica Ebenezer

They are only a small church with about 140 members. They broadcast three one-hour long messages each week to forty-two countries and seven states in Spain. One station is in Georgia, USA! They have other ministries, such as a large Bible distribution, [and] a program with clothing and other necessities. In addition, they have drug and alcohol recovery programs, and their pastor has *two part-time jobs*!

Carla and I met a sweet young mother and daughter from Ecuador. The mother's name is Angela and she helped us interpret. Later we found out that she wasn't a member of the church, but evidently joined after her visit with us today. Afterwards, we all ate at a little Spanish restaurante and took the train back to the hotel.

13

Retiro Park

First time for the gospel being preached openly!

May 11, 2002 Saturday
Prayed in the middle of the night over an hour. In the morning, I read Proverbs 11. This chapter, I believe, focuses on righteousness, which is right standing before God. The verse that spoke to me concerning our calling for this trip to Spain was verse 30: "The fruit of the righteous is a tree of life; and he who wins souls is wise" (NKJV). The Holy Spirit confirmed it in numerous ways. Later, at lunch, Karen (at Burger King) brought up a question about righteousness which turned into a nice devotional finished up with prayer.

We bus toured in the a.m. In the late afternoon, after the rain stopped, we all went to Retiro Park where many Ecuadorians hang out. We brought trinkets, puppets, a little candy, and bubble jars. Then, we took their pictures with a Polaroid camera and gave them out. When we had quite a crowd in one area, the Lord told us to preach the gospel to them. We started out by singing a couple of songs. All of this was spontaneous. Then, Shirley started, and I raising my voice so all could hear, finished presenting the gospel to them, with Keely interpreting. This was a *first* for Keely. I told the people that we had come all this way for one purpose: to tell them about Jesus and what He could do for them. I also quoted two of my memorized salvation verses in Spanish, John 3:16 and John 1:12. They were all attentive, Keely interpreted several other verses, including Romans 10:9–13. After this, I asked all who wanted to receive Jesus as their Lord and Savior to bow their heads and repeat a prayer and mean it in their hearts. Numerous ones, we believe hundreds, bowed their heads and prayed! Thank You Lord! Afterwards, we all sang a hymn verse and passed out our few remaining tracts and followed up with a few folks.

We found out later from the missionaries that *no one has ever been allowed to openly preach the gospel in Spain*! The missionaries weren't trained for this, only to pass out tracts and Bibles and privately share the gospel and witness. Thank the Lord for opening the door (Revelation 3:7–8).

14

Key of David

Saturday, May 11, 2002

Continued *Revelation 3:7* and *8*.

> "These things saith he that is holy, he that is true, he that hath the key of David, he that openeth, and no man shutteth, and shutteth, and no man openeth; (8)I know thy works: behold, I have set before thee an open door, and no man can shut it: for thou hast a little strength, and hast kept my word, and hast not denied my name." (KJV)

We continue to pray for Madrid, everyone here.

We had a run in with pickpockets who tried to rob all of us, but were unsuccessful. Despite the rain, mishaps on the escalator and train door, and pickpockets, it's been a glorious day. Thank you, Lord!

Sunday, Domingo, May 12, 2002 7:30 a.m.

Prayed forty-five minutes, then read a little from Isaiah; I also read Proverbs 12 and John 3. Church service at Ebenezer Comunidad Christian Church was more than excellent! It's a dynamic Spanish-speaking church. Pastor Joaquin Yebra Serro used my Spanish-English KJV Bible to preach from in both languages! His text was John 11. I mentioned this church earlier. At this service, I was honored as the pastor asked me to close the service in prayer.

After lunch at McDonald's, we went to Retiro Park and witnessed and ministered to scores of Ecuadorian immigrants. We passed out trinkets and toys and shared Jesus's love. We didn't seem to have the degree of freedom there as we had yesterday. We met another team of Americans there, mostly students from a Baptist college in California. We also met the man and his wife in charge of the area's missionaries for the immigrants: Rusti and Patti.

We all had a nice supper at the Chicago Restaurant, then took the Metro back to the Chamartin Hotel. I stayed up sending out postcards and logging this. Thank you, Lord, for another great day!

15

Castle

Monday, May 13, 2002

Got up early after staying up late. In the morning, we all ate an early breakfast, then took the train to Segovia. It was a beautiful scenic ride there. It turned out to be an extremely picturesque city, old medieval style, with King Ferdinand and Queen Isabella's castle. A Roman aqueduct, cathedrals, and old shops, etc. We took many pictures. I went to the top of the castle, leaned over the roof, and prayed for all of Spain from there. Scanning over miles of scenery, snowcapped mountains and Spanish-style homes and buildings, I was reminded of Jesus when the devil took Him to a high mountain and showed Him in a moment all the kingdoms of the world. Who was the devil kidding? They already belonged to Jesus! "The earth is the Lord's, and the fulness thereof; the world, and they that dwell therein" (Psalm 24:1KJV).

Later, we shopped for souvenirs: a small vase, a wooden box for my Bible verses with an old-world map on it, two necklaces for myself and Carla, and four T-shirts for the boys. In the evening, I read Matthew 5 and 6:5 (Beatitudes and kingdom living), Matthew 6 regarding prayer (including the Lord's prayer verses 9–13). Also, about heavenly virtues and rewards.

16

Still Small Voice

Tuesday May 14, 2002

Prayed in the middle of the night briefly. I had an exhausting day yesterday physically. In the a.m. read 1 Kings 19 about Elijah fleeing for his life. He sat under a juniper tree and had a pity party. He was tired, afraid, and depressed. He rested. An angel touched him, and he ate…then, on a mountain in a cave. The Lord was not in the earthquake, wind, or fire, but a still small voice (a delicate whispering voice)! God told Elijah to anoint two kings and Elisha. Notice the necessity of the anointing. God doesn't shout. We, His children, need to pray for ears to hear and discern His still small voice!

17

Parla

In the morning, we all traveled to the nearby small town of Parla, where we met Bill, one of the Southern Baptist missionaries. We all split up and prayer walked. We prayed especially for the church there. Earlier in the restaurant, I had made an off the wall comment about "small sized portions." Later, as we were prayer walking, we passed three small men (or dwarfs). We also passed a mother and son who were friendly. I talked to the mother, Delaura, at length (with my broken Spanish; she knew no English). Her son's name is Alexander (pronounced Alehondro). She's a student at a university in Madrid. I believe she is a Jehovah's Witness. When I gave her a tract, she gave me a Jehovah's Witness tract. I quoted John 3:16 to her in Español. Delaura asked what time the church service was, and I told her.

Afterward, we all had lunch at a Moroccan restaurant. The people who ran and owned the restaurant were friends of Bill. He's been working just since February, making inroads in their religion. The food was scrumptious, and they were very friendly.

Later, Carla and I, and Karla and Ruth went to the bullfight at the world-famous Plaza De Toros Las Ventas, the most prestigious bullring in the world. We saw *three* bulls killed, and then left.

Tuesday, May 14, 2002 (continued)

More 3s; today it's ironic!

In my Bible study (1) earthquake (2) wind and, (3) fire *3* anointings from Elijah; *3* dwarfs, *3* missionaries we worked with; *3* Euro dollars in change from the bullfight; *3* matadors plunged *3* sets of darts (swords) into each bull; *3* black bulls killed. In Parla, we saw *3* black swans in a fountain. Later, when Carla told the ladies about the many threes, they said more sets of 3s happened to them, at least thirteen 3s! I looked up the biblical meaning for *three*: conform (obey; imitate).[1] (1) God/The Godhead (2) complete (3) resurrection; (4) perfect (8) witness.

---

[1] Adam F. Thompson and Adrian Beale, *The Divinity Code to Understanding Your Dreams and Visions* (Shippensburg, PA: Destiny Image Publishers, 2011), page.

18

Spiritual Warfare

Wednesday May 15, 2002

Prayed in the middle of the night over half an hour in the morning. Breakfast with Carla at the hotel. Afterwards, the ladies, including Carla, went to the Plaza Mayor to see the dancers and to shop. I read some of Luke 23 and Acts 17. I picked up our pictures, and confirmed our flight times, then took a nap.

At around 1:00 p.m., I prayed for Carla and the missionaries with her. Later, I found out that pickpockets tried to steal from the ladies at that time but were unsuccessful. Thank you, Lord. After lunch, I came back to the room and read more of the book *Spiritual Warfare* by Richard Ing. I then prayed much for Madrid.

I prayed against the various strongmen/powers of evil in the heavenlies over this city, binding them and drying up their waters, smashing their gates, cutting off their cords and tentacles from the enslaved souls below and casting out demons with the blood of Jesus and the Word of God. I'm still praying for over 1,000,000 souls to be saved soon here in Madrid. Thank you, Lord!

19

Mission Accomplished

Wednesday May 15, 2002 continued

Later in the day, the missionaries Dana, Karen, Keeley, Shirley, Sandy, Ruth, Karla, Carla, and I went out for a farewell supper. We all filled out questionnaires, exchanged addresses, and phone numbers. We took pictures and shared highlights of the trip and prayed. We all agreed that it was a very successful, God blessed trip! Dana and Keeley said the gospel had never been preached openly to a public group here before or with so much freedom! The bottom line: *many souls* were saved, and many more seeds of the gospel were sown, all because of God's love and grace in calling all of us here and answering our prayers!

We were able to win many souls to the Lord, by God's grace. Additionally, I, who was good as dead inside and unable to conceive children until this time, was able to get my wife, Carla, pregnant. Thank You, Lord! I was fifty-four, and Carla was forty-one years old. Thank you, Father God! In Jesus's name, Amen!

20

Adios España

Thursday, May 16, 2002
Got up early for the plane trip home. We said our goodbyes to everyone. Keely went with us to the airport, then we began our long journey home. I had lots of time to catch up on my reading. Read *Fresh Power* by Jim Cymbala. Thank you, Lord for seeing us safely all the way home!

21

Good News! Elijah

Monday, July 1, 2002

Carla had the first indications that she was pregnant. Wednesday, July 4, 2002 I took Carla into the emergency room due to cramping and pains. They tested her and said she would be all right and confirmed she was pregnant (seven weeks and four days along). This was at 2:30 a.m. She was able to see and hear the baby's heartbeat on the monitor! "Behold, children are a heritage from the Lord, the fruit of the womb is a (his-KJV) reward" (Psalm 127:3 NKJV). Seven months later, February 20, 2003, baby Elijah was born. Praise the Lord!

Addendum

In conclusion, summarizing our journey, I would say that our sovereign God called and chose nine missionaries at this time, and in His way, saved many souls and touched countless lives in Spain and elsewhere, for His Kingdom and glory!

All glory be to God,
Terence and C. Lewis

40

The Wonder of His Love

Terry and Carla Lewis © July 28, 2016

The love of God sees us; the love of God frees us;

The love of God shows us; the wonder of His love!

Love knows no end, It has no bounds; It reaches where all sin is found; Its healing balm comes from above; Nothing moves us like His love! Nothing moves us like His love.

The love of God sees us; the love of God frees us;

The love of God shows us; the wonder of His love!

Love forgives and transforms lives; liberates and satisfies; It bears, believes, hopes and endures;

Unfailing love, prevailing cure. Unfailing love, prevailing cure.

The love of God sees us; the love of God frees us; the love of God shows us;

The wonder of His love!

Who can know the depth the height; Our Father loves with *all* His might; from His love we'll never part; for we are kept within His heart. Yes, we are kept within His heart.

The love of God sees us; the love of God frees us; the love of God shows us;

The wonder of His love! The wonder of His love!

Love sent His Son, the only one; His life to give that we might live; only believe, and Him

Receive; you'll know the wonder of God's love! You'll know the wonder of His love.

Because of God's wondrous love, we were privileged not only to experience it ourselves, but to share it with others!

Bibliography

Thompson, Adam F. and Adrian Beale. *The Divinity Code to Understanding Your Dreams and Visions.* Shippensburg, PA: Destiny Image Publishers, 2011.

Printed in the United States
by Baker & Taylor Publisher Services